The Wogglebug's Book of Manners

Copyright © 2025 by Cynthia Hanson

Printed in the U.S.A.
Exclusively for WogglebugLove Productions.

First Edition: September 2025
ISBN: 9780615818061

(WogglebugLove Productions)

The Wogglebug's Book of Manners.

by Cynthia Hanson

WogglebugLove Productions

Hello to all of you, my dear young friends! It gives me such pleasure to see you all today! Now as you must have noticed, I am a thoroughly educated gentlebug with the manners of such. I learned them all by listening to and observing the wise professor and also his students in the school room I had grown up in, so to speak. And now as I am a teacher myself I shall be honored to give you a lesson on how to have the manners I have, which are easy and fun to learn. So you just listen to and observe me as I go through a whole day that is typical for me in the Land of Genoma.

I wake up along with the rising of the sun, as I do every day to remind myself to be always happy and alert to all around me with a good grace. Then as I step out of my room and enter the hall on my way out I come across three dignitaries, Hulan, Sprague, and Reynolds. I calmly walk by them and let them not notice me as I know they'd rather not. These fellows will eventually come around, until then I'll just let them act like they don't know me.

I walk towards a very particular spot outside the castle. Then after a moment, Sylvie comes out from the portal from her own world. Then she and at once give each other hugs. And giving hugs are my favorite kinds of manners. For they are the manners for saying "I love you."

Sylvie and I meet with the Frogman. Sylvie hugs him and I let the Frogman know also about how much his friendship will always mean to me. Then the Frogman says the same to me and congratulates Sylvie on her year of happiness as our friend.

We soon decide to go on a picnic together. I carry the basket and along our way we come by the five little clowns as they go along hopping and skipping down the path. We pause and allow them to pass in front of us. They invite us to come to their talent show at the castle this evening. I assure them we would love to. I tip my hat and we all wave to them.

Once we reach the spot for our picnic we spread out our blanket and set up our meal together. I sit up straight beside Sylvie and the Frogman. When I want something I always ask with "please," and then reply with 'thank you' when it is given to me. I sometimes reply with 'no thank you' when they ask if I want something. I also never speak with my mouth full and I also use my napkin.

After our picnic we clean up around us and then we decide we want to go to the Enchanted Forest to visit our friends there. Along our way we meet with a few Wise Old Oaks. They are the speakers of ancient wisdom. They tell us "Life be not so short but there is always time for courtesy."

We enter the village of the forest elves and meet with Christeph. He is happy to see us and shows us his new trees and bushes that grow candies and cookies. He explains he wasn't sure how his new invention would be received. I assure him he is a genius and should be proud of his achievement. He picks one of the cookies off a tree and offers it to me. After I bite into it I let him know how good it is.

Shortly afterward, our friend Theodora the pixie leader flies over. She informs us the Troll Wizards Fashzam and Sarahem need us quickly. As she flies up she scatters her pixie dust and it causes me to sneeze. But I always cover my nose and mouth with my handkerchief and this prevents me offending her.

We find the Troll Wizards who are in the middle of a dispute about a spell. Which is not uncommon for those two. So after I say, "Pardon me, my friends!" I just explain to them that it is alright for them to disagree as long as they respect each other's personal boundaries.

The Troll Wizards were then able to easily resolve their quarrel. And they cast their spell. Which it turned out was a spell to turn the giant mushrooms surrounding us into giant butterflies. We are all delighted to see them.

Later on the way to the castle I come across another two close friends of mine. Princess Rachel and her live teddy bear companion, Randy. I smile and say "Good evening" to them. Then I learn they are on their way to the castle also for the talent show tonight to participate. I smile and wish them good luck during it.

Once I was back in the castle, I began to prepare myself for the party this evening. And who isn't always concerned with how they look and act at a party, especially when it is here in the castle? So after I had washed myself up and had my clothes neatly pressed to perfection, I headed out to the dining room.

As everyone was gathering inside and the party was beginning, I greeted as many of the other guests as I could who came by me and I gave them my best smile, letting them know how happy I was to see them here also.

When I at one point end up bumping into Zoey the little dragon I quickly stand back and say, "Oh! Pardon me! I didn't see you there a moment ago!" Zoey smiles and nods and mentions how he is performing in the show tonight with his puppy band. I smile and assure him he will do well and will be a joy to watch.

Once dinner was served I sat beside the Frogman and Sylvie. I followed the same etiquette as I had at the picnic. I sat up straight, and ate politely, I would never interrupt when someone else was speaking, and of course I always used my napkin.

Then when the show begins I take my seat next to the others. I am a good watcher and I always sit still and never speak. Although I like to laugh and applaud when the time is right for it, of course. I am so impressed by all I see I decide next year I will try out for the talent show.

Afterwards, the dance begins. I take Sylvie's hand and bow as I dance with her. As she leads I compliment her on the fancy gown she is wearing.

After this, everyone began to slowly leave. And just before my friends and I went our separate ways we hugged and said good night to each other. I mentioned to them I had a very grand day with them, and I appreciated them for just being who they are.

Well, that is all for now. Goodbye, my young friends, and I hope you've all enjoyed hearing this lesson as much as I have enjoyed giving it.

To Find out more visit
https://www.wogglebugloveproductions.com

www.ingramcontent.com/pod-product-compliance
Lightning Source LLC
Chambersburg PA
CBHW042113040426

42448CB00002B/246

9780615818061